Managing Editor
Mara Ellen Guckian

Editor in Chief
Karen J. Goldfluss, M.S. Ed.

Creative Director
Sarah M. Fournier

Cover Artist
Diem Pascarella

Art Coordinator
Renée Mc Elwee

Illustrator
Kelly McMahon

Imaging
James Edward Grace

Publisher
Mary D. Smith, M.S. Ed.

TCR 8004

All About SUPER Me!

This Journal Belongs To

Author
Mara Ellen Guckian

Teacher Created Resources
12621 Western Avenue
Garden Grove, CA 92841
www.teachercreated.com
ISBN: 978-1-4206-8004-1

©2017 Teacher Created Resources
Reprinted, 2020

Made in U.S.A.

Teacher Created Resources

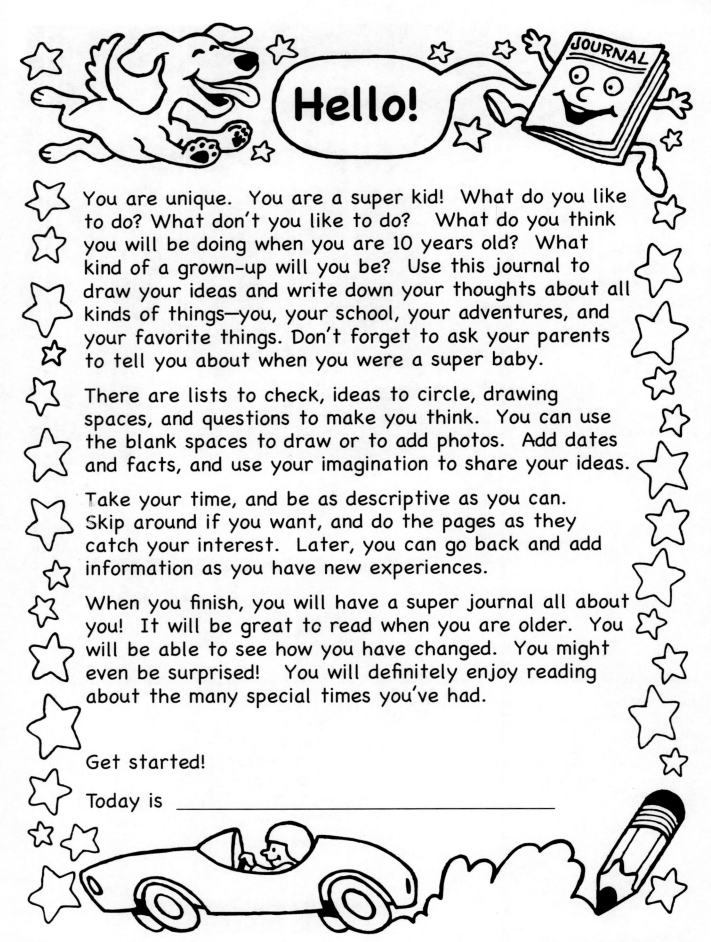

Hello!

You are unique. You are a super kid! What do you like to do? What don't you like to do? What do you think you will be doing when you are 10 years old? What kind of a grown-up will you be? Use this journal to draw your ideas and write down your thoughts about all kinds of things—you, your school, your adventures, and your favorite things. Don't forget to ask your parents to tell you about when you were a super baby.

There are lists to check, ideas to circle, drawing spaces, and questions to make you think. You can use the blank spaces to draw or to add photos. Add dates and facts, and use your imagination to share your ideas.

Take your time, and be as descriptive as you can. Skip around if you want, and do the pages as they catch your interest. Later, you can go back and add information as you have new experiences.

When you finish, you will have a super journal all about you! It will be great to read when you are older. You will be able to see how you have changed. You might even be surprised! You will definitely enjoy reading about the many special times you've had.

Get started!

Today is _____

Introducing... Super Me!

Here is a picture of me!

I am ⬜ years old.

The best thing about being my age is _____

_____

_____

 # About My Name

My first name is _____.

My middle name is _____.

My last name is _____.

I am usually called

_____.

My mom's name is

_____.

My dad's name is

_____.

If I had picked my name, it would be _____.

I like that name because _____

_____.

The Day I Was Born

The Date: I was born on _____ .

That date is now my birthday!

The Place: I was born in _____ .

city,   state   or   country

The Time of Day: ☐ daytime   ☐ nighttime

The Season: I was born in the

Winter ☐

Spring ☐

Summer ☐

Fall ☐

My STATS

Weight

I weighed _____ pounds _____ ounces.

Length

I was _____ inches long.

My Hair Then

I had ☐ no hair ☐ some hair ☐ a lot of hair

My Family Then

I had [ ] brothers and [ ] sisters when I was born.

Now, I have [ ] brothers and [ ] sisters.

More Information

When I was born, _____

_____

When I Was Little

I have heard stories about when I was little.

I had a special _____.

I liked _____.

This is a picture of me then. I was _____.

I have learned to do many things since I was born. I am glad I learned to

_____

_____.

I Am Growing

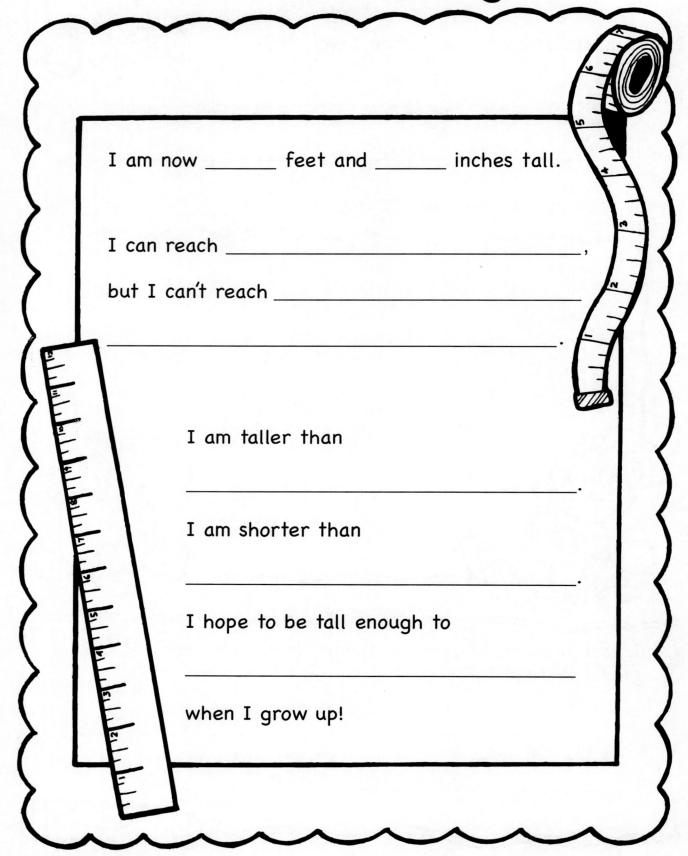

I am now _____ feet and _____ inches tall.

I can reach _____,

but I can't reach _____

_____.

I am taller than

_____.

I am shorter than

_____.

I hope to be tall enough to

_____

when I grow up!

Me, My Eyes, and My Hair

Eyes

My eyes are ☐ blue ☐ green ☐ brown ☐ hazel

☐ I wear glasses.

☐ I do not wear glasses.

Hair

My Hair

My hair is

☐ black

☐ brown

☐ blond

☐ red

☐ other

My hair is

☐ very long

☐ long

☐ medium

☐ short

☐ very short

My hair is ☐ Curly ☐ Wavy ☐ Straight

 # My Family

There are _____ people in my family. They are important to me.

This is a picture of us. I have added everyone's names and ages.

My family on my mom's side is from _____.

My family on my dad's side is from _____.

My favorite thing to do with my family is _____

_____.

More Super People

I am lucky. I have other super people in my life, too. Here are pictures of two people who are very special in my life.

_____ is

special to me because

_____.

_____ is

special to me because

_____.

My Home

I have colored the kind of home that is the most like mine.

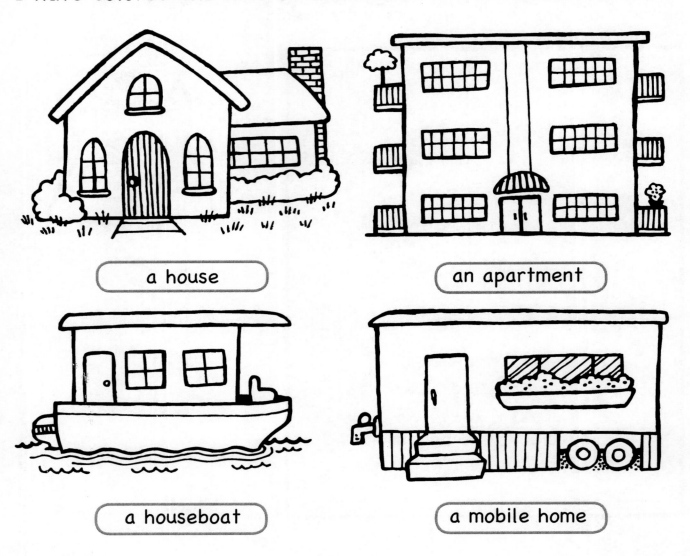

a house

an apartment

a houseboat

a mobile home

My Home

The best thing about my home is _____.

My favorite room in my home is _____

because _____

_____.

Where I Live

This is my address.

Street _____

City _____

State _____

Country _____

I live near or by

☐ the mountains.

☐ a desert.

☐ a valley.

☐ a beach.

☐ a city.

When I grow up I want to live near _____

so that I can _____ .

Our Weather

I have circled what the weather is like where I live. I have added something I like to do and something I wear in each season.

Where I live, the weather changes

☐ a lot   ☐ some   ☐ not much

SEASON	WEATHER	
Summer I like to _____. I wear _____.	hot warm cold	sunny snowy rainy
Fall I like to _____. I wear _____.	hot warm cold	sunny snowy rainy
Winter I like to _____. I wear _____.	hot warm cold	sunny snowy rainy
Spring I like to _____. I wear _____.	hot warm cold	sunny snowy rainy

School Is Important

I go to _____ School.

I am in _____. I have been going to school for _____ years.
  grade

There are _____ kids in my class.

boys	girls

To get to school, I ☐ walk.

☐ ride a bike.

☐ take a ferry.

☐ take a bus.

☐ ride in a car/carpool.

☐ other _____

My teacher's name is _____.

My teacher likes to _____.

I am lucky because my teacher is _____.

School Days

I go to school so that I can _____.

My favorite part of the school day is _____.

My favorite thing to do at recess is _____.

My two favorite subjects are

☐ Art

☐ Computer

☐ Math

☐ Music

☐ Reading

☐ Science

☐ Social Studies

☐ _____

I wish we could do more _____ at school

because _____.

My Friends

Having friends is important. These are some of my friends' names:

_____   _____   _____

When I am playing with one friend, I like to _____

_____ .

When I am with a group of friends, we like to _____

_____ .

I try to be a good friend. I try to _____

_____ .

My Friends

A Super School Day

Sometimes we do special things at school.

One thing I really like is when we _____.

The best day of school so far was the day we _____

_____.

It was great because _____.

A Super Day

I Am Happy...

When I am happy, I _____ .

I have written and drawn things in my web that make me happy.

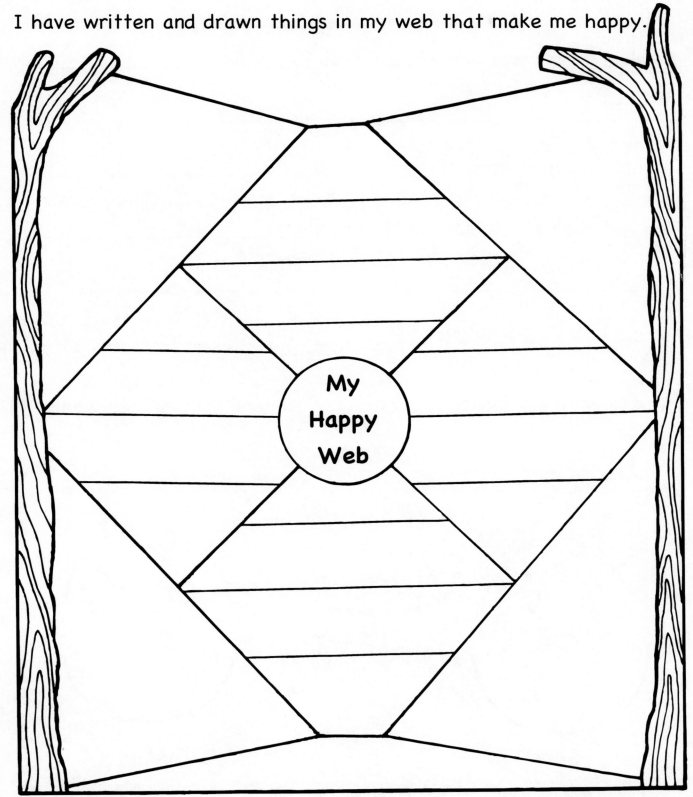

My Happy Web

Sad or Mad

Sometimes I am, sad and sometimes I get mad.

The last time I was *sad* was because _____

_____ .

To feel better, I tried to _____ .

The last time I was *mad* was because _____

_____ .

To feel better, I tried to _____ .

This is what my mouth looks like for some of the feelings I have.

Sad   Happy   Mad

What Color Is Happy?

If I had to choose a color for every feeling, I would color the crayons this way.

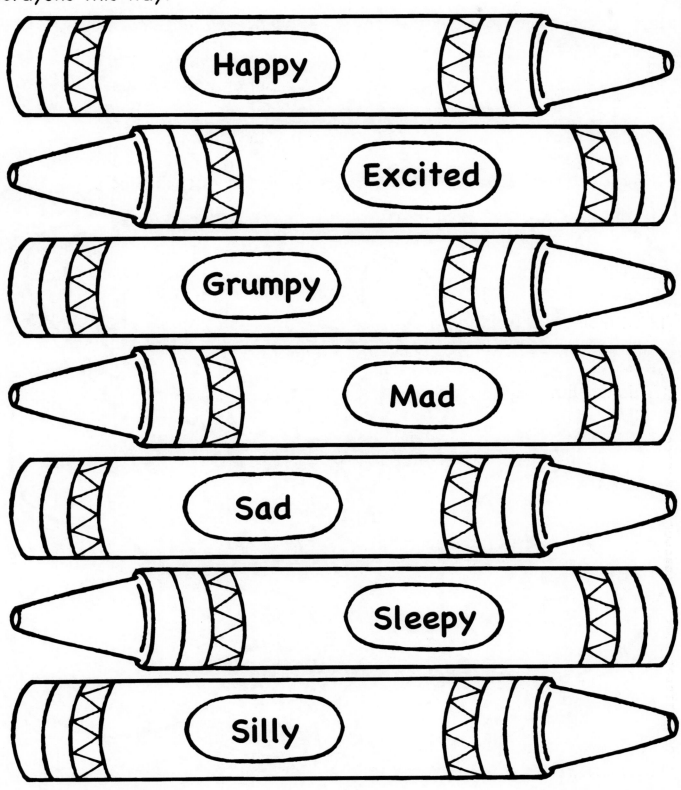

I Am Grateful

To be *grateful* means to be *thankful*.

Here are some of the ways I try to show that I am grateful.

☐ I say thank you.   ☐ I share my things.

☐ I help out.   ☐ I give hugs.

I have written something I am grateful for in each balloon.

I Am a Helper

The older I get, the more I can help. Here are some ways I try to be helpful.

At Home

At School

At the Park

One thing I need help with is_____ .

A Better Place

It is important to help make our world a better place.

♡ I have checked some ways that I will help.

☐ Be kind to others.

☐ Don't litter.

☐ Donate toys and books.

☐ Donate used clothes.

☐ Plant a tree or a garden.

☐ Recycle and reuse.

☐ Save water.

♡ Here is what I can do right now.

_____

Things I Like to Do

This is a super list of things to do. I have put a check mark by each thing I like to do. I also circled four of my favorites!

- art projects
- build things
- cook
- dance
- do gymnastics
- do puzzles
- draw
- garden
- go bike riding
- go hiking
- go ice-skating
- go roller-skating

- paint
- play board games
- play card games
- play computer games
- play sports
- read
- run
- sing
- skateboard
- swim
- take pictures
- write stories

Games, Games, Games!

There are so many different kinds of games. Here are the names of some games that I enjoy playing.

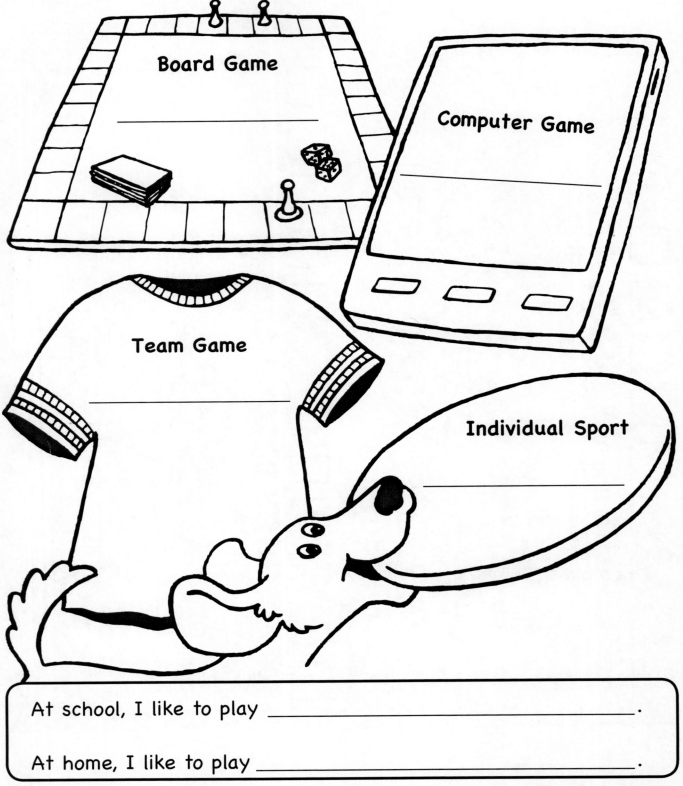

Board Game

_____

Computer Game

_____

Team Game

_____

Individual Sport

_____

At school, I like to play _____.

At home, I like to play _____.

 # My Favorite Foods

Fruits _____ _____

Vegetables _____ _____

Cereals _____ _____

Drinks _____ _____

Here are my favorite foods for each meal.

Breakfast

Dinner

Lunch

And finally, here are my favorite treats!

My Favorite Holidays

Holidays are fun! Some holidays are times for families and friends to get together. Others celebrate special events. Here are two of my favorites. I drew pictures of things we do on each holiday.

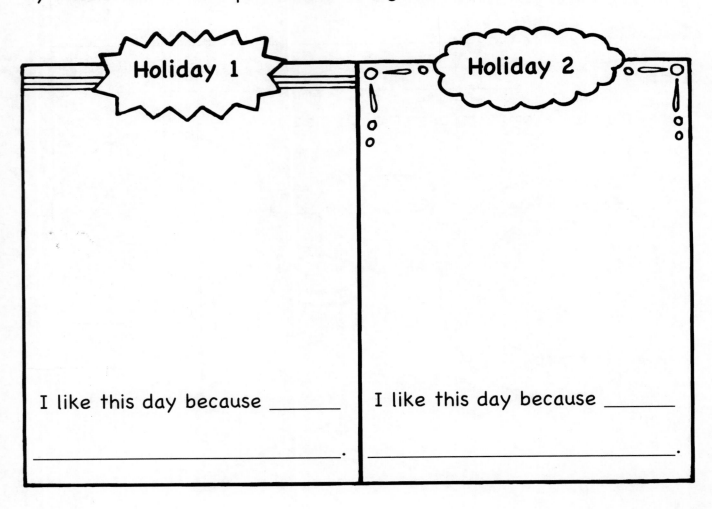

Holiday 1

I like this day because _____

_____ .

Holiday 2

I like this day because _____

_____ .

My birthday is also a special day.

Here is a cake I decorated. I also added candles to show how old I will be on my **next** birthday.

Pets

Here is a list of pets. I have checked the ones I would like to have someday. I circled the pets I have now.

☐ bird

☐ cat

☐ dog

☐ fish

☐ frog

☐ hermit crab

☐ horse

☐ lizard

☐ rabbit

☐ snake

☐ turtle

☐ other _____

I think the most amazing animal to have as a pet would be a

_____ .

This is a picture of my dream pet and me.

I would feed it

_____ .

It would sleep

_____ .

Animal Favorites

There are all kinds of animals in the world. I am going to draw my favorite animal in each group.

Farm Animal

Forest Animal

Jungle Animal

Ocean Animal

Music I Like

I like to ☐ sing. ☐ listen to music.

☐ dance. ☐ play an instrument.

I play music loud when I am _____.

I play music softly when I am _____.

Here are some of my favorites in music. I may put more than one favorite on a line because it is too hard to choose.

Favorite Singer _____

Favorite Group _____

Favorite Song _____

Favorite Musical Instrument

I play _____.

Someday I might like to play _____.

I Can Read!

I like to read books about _____.

☐ I like to hold a book when I read.

☐ I like to read books online.

For me, the best place to read is_____

The book character I would like to be is_____

because _____

_____.

If I ever write a book, I think it will be about

_____

_____

_____

_____.

The cover might look like this.

My Favorite Book

My all-time favorite book was written by

_____ .

The title is _____

_____ .

This book is special to me because _____

_____

_____ .

Here is a picture of my favorite part.

TV and Movies

TV

My favorite TV show is _____

because _____ .

My favorite character on TV is _____

because _____ .

If I could star **in my own** TV show, it would be about

_____ .

Movies

I loved the movie _____ .

It made me feel _____ .

My favorite part was _____

_____ .

If I could be a character in a movie I have seen,
I would be

_____ .

Traveling

To *travel* means to go from one place to another.

The farthest I have traveled is to _____.

Sometimes I walk or hike. I have circled the other ways I have traveled.

| bike | boat | bus |
| motorcycle |
| car | ferry | motorcycle |
| plane | submarine | train |

My favorite way to travel so far is _____.

Someday, I want to travel by _____.

 A Very Exciting Trip

The most exciting trip I have ever taken was to _____

_____.

I went with _____.

It was a

☐ day trip.   ☐ trip to visit family.

☐ family vacation.   ☐ "spur of the moment" idea.

We traveled by _____.

We saw _____.

We ate _____.

We got to _____.

Day Trips

Sometimes, we take day trips to special places. Here are two day trips I have really enjoyed.

Trip 1

I went to_____.

While I was there, I_____.

The best part of this trip was_____

_____

_____.

Trip 2

I went to_____.

While I was there, I_____.

The best part of this trip was_____

_____

_____.

My Perfect Day

I would spend my perfect day at _____ .

It would be ☐ **Summer** ☐ **Fall** ☐ **Winter** ☐ **Spring**

The weather would be _____ .

I would wear

_____

_____

_____

I would bring

_____

_____

_____

Here is a picture of me on my perfect day!

When I Grow Up

When I grow up I might want to be a _____

or a _____ .

doctor

computer game designer

If I am a _____

writer

I would get to _____ .

artist

To do this, I will need to learn more about

pizza delivery person

_____

rock star

I would use these tools at my job:

horse trainer

_____ _____ _____

actor

If I am a _____

astronaut

I would get to _____ .

teacher

To do this, I will need to learn more about

baseball player

_____ .

dog groomer

police officer

I would use these tools at my job:

_____ _____ _____

Dreams

Sometimes when you sleep, you dream.

I think I remember my dreams ☐ all the time.

☐ some of the time.

Once, in a dream I _____

_____ .

My Dream

Short, Tall, or Invisible

If I were only 3 inches tall,
I would be as tall as this box!

I could _____

_____ .

But I could not _____

_____ .

If I were a giant, I'd
be as tall as a

_____ .

I could _____

_____ .

But I could not

_____ .

If I were invisible, no one could see me.

The good part of being invisible would be

_____ .

The bad part of being invisible would be

_____ .

If I could choose to be one way for a day, I would like to be

☐ 3 inches tall   ☐ a giant   ☐ invisible

Inventions Are Tools

Inventions help make jobs easier. Some are simple tools, like a toothbrush or a fork. Other inventions have moving parts, like cars and washing machines.

I use inventions every day. Here are two that help me.

1. _____

2. _____

I would like to invent a _____ .

It would make it easier to _____ .

My invention might look like this:

 # If I Lived in the Ocean

If I could be an ocean animal, I would be _____

_____.

I chose this animal because_____

_____.

I would live in   I would live

☐ cold water.   ☐ near the shore.

☐ warm water.   ☐ deep in the ocean.

This is a picture of what it would be like.

If I Could Fly

If I could fly I would like to

☐ have wings all the time.

☐ wear a jet pack I could take on and off.

I would be able to go _____

_____ .

The best part would be _____

_____ .

Look at Me Fly!

 # If I Built a Robot

My robot would be able to _____.

It would have _____

and a special _____.

My robot would be called _____.

I would control it with

☐ my voice.   ☐ a remote control.

Here is a picture of my robot.

My Hideout

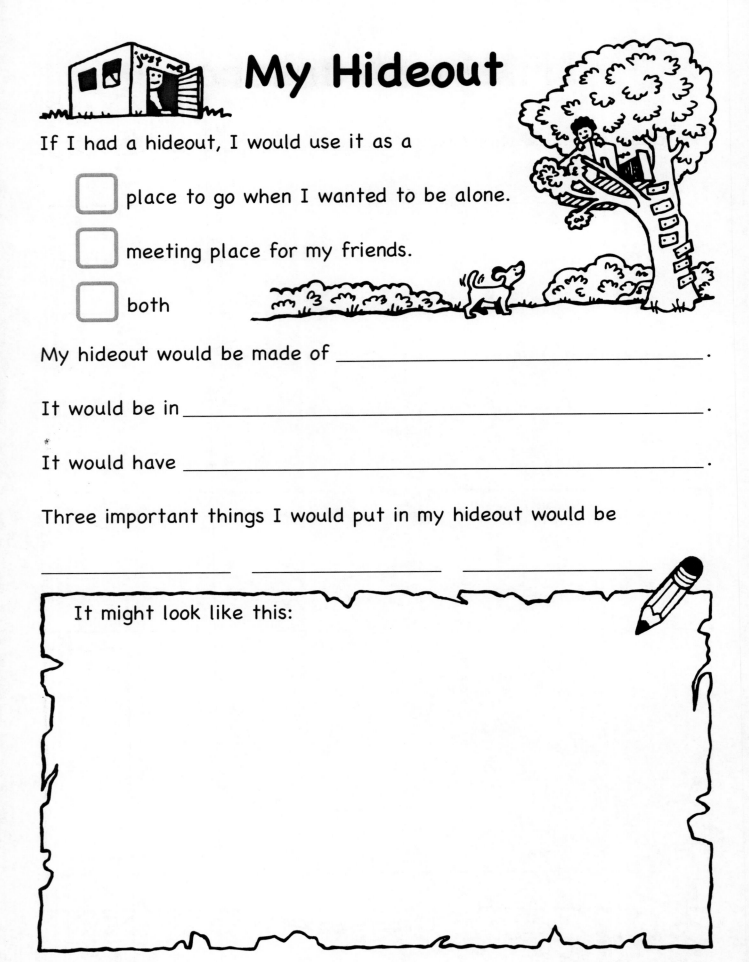

If I had a hideout, I would use it as a

☐ place to go when I wanted to be alone.

☐ meeting place for my friends.

☐ both

My hideout would be made of _____.

It would be in _____.

It would have _____.

Three important things I would put in my hideout would be

_____   _____   _____

It might look like this:

Find a Treasure

If I could only pick one, I would like to find

☐ a treasure at the end of the rainbow.

☐ a genie who could grant me one wish.

☐ a leprechaun with a pot of gold.

☐ a goose that lays golden eggs.

☐ a fairy godmother.

Then I could _____

_____.

Draw your treasure!

My Super Dreams

If I could make a dream come true for my family, I would

wish for

_____

because _____

_____.

If I could make a wish for the world, I would wish _____

_____.

It would help _____

_____.